ordinary sparkling moments

Reflections on Success and Contentment

Christine MASON Miller ✳ ✳ ✳

FORWARD BY KERI SMITH

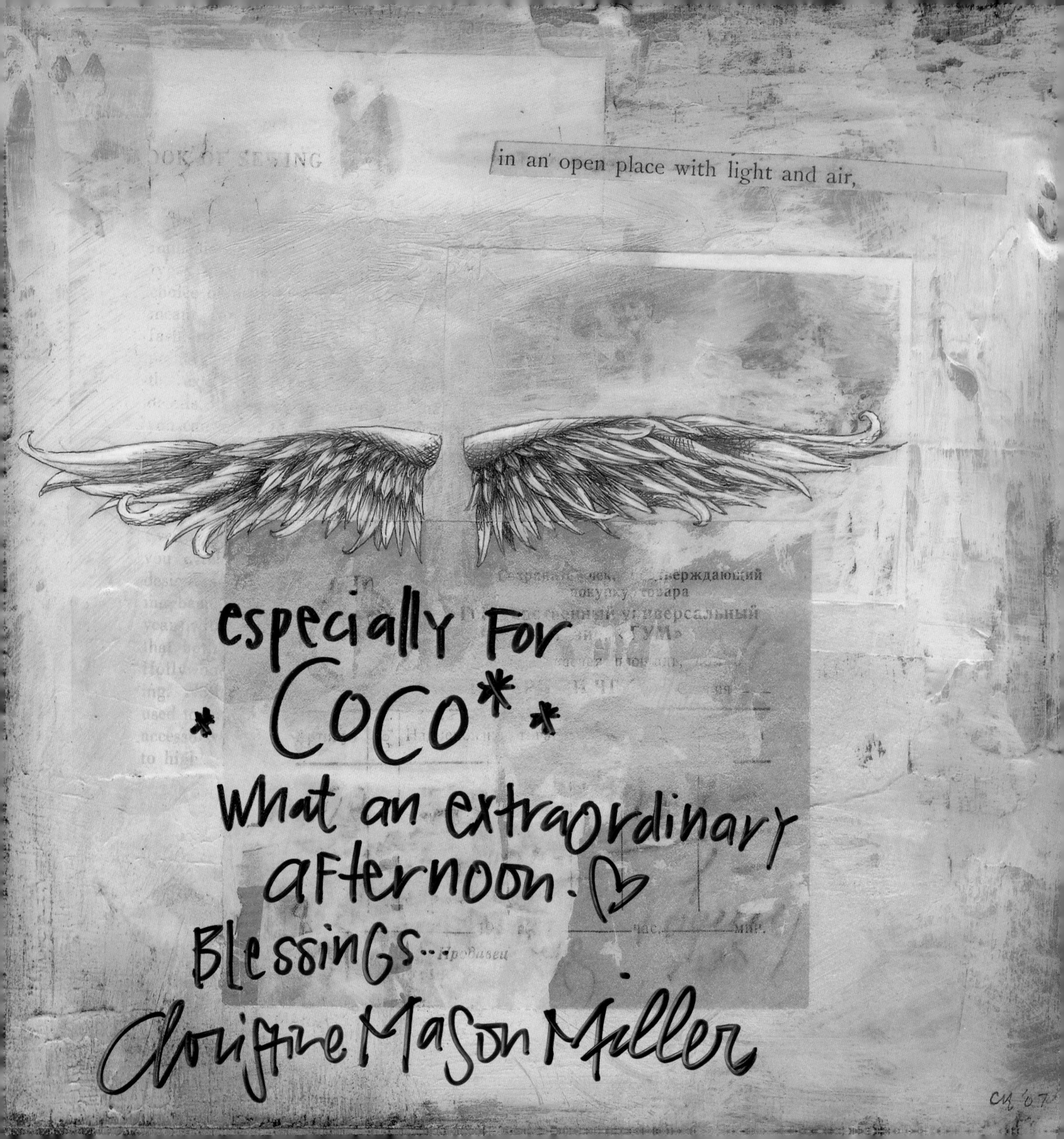
in an open place with light and air,
especially For
* Coco * *
What an extraordinary
afternoon. ♡
Blessings...
Christine Mason Miller
CM '07

'05 Lawrence

Who is John Galt?

Forward

Many years ago I came to know about Christine (aka Swirly) through a network of creative souls who had connected via the online world, each of us experimenting with this new medium as a means to share our process with the world. I was drawn to Christine because there was a certain energy and life to her writings. She demonstrated an Intense passion for life, an unwavering gratitude for the people and gifts she had been given, and the photos on her blog presented a woman who was strong, invincible, and always surrounded by color. There was something about her that was magnetic, yet I remember feeling that her work seemed to sit on the surface of who she really was, something I had seen in myself in recent months. I silently wondered what lurked below the surface, yet I was aware in that moment that it was not quite time for us to connect. Somehow I knew that when the time was right I would know.

A few years later I visited her site after not having done so for many months. I immediately noticed a new intensity to her writing, a rawness and a longing that had not been there before, and this echoed something in my own life — the kind of VULNERABILITY that comes from going through hell and living to tell the TALE. I found myself smiling uncontrollably, and I knew at that moment it was time to connect.

My first email to her went something like this↴

Dear Christine,
I know you don't know me but I have been reading your site for a few years now and I sense that you have been through a big life change lately. One that has made your work and your writing more real. And while I can't say exactly why this is I just want to tell you that I noticed. And it's beautiful. I thank you greatly for sharing it because I see parts of myself in you and I am growing because of it.
Creatively yours, Keri Smith

She wrote back immediately telling me that I was exactly right, and that because of the depths of her experience she was finally coming into the person she was meant to be. It was this exchange that began a deep friendship built on sharing our truths and encouraging each other to be more authentic versions of ourselves.

As artists we are propelled forward by our innate curiosity and unfailing need to question the world around us. On both a personal and a societal level we take on the role of holding a mirror up to ourselves and the world and reflecting back a multitude of truths, but these truths can only be shared after we have faced our own dark places.

In this book Christine asks us "WHAT DOES IT MEAN TO LIVE AN AUTHENTIC LIFE?" By sharing some of her thoughts and experiences she attempts to peel away the layers of the CREATED SELF in search of what it means to live fully open to what gives us the greatest meaning, even when that is extremely challenging. In doing so, she gives us permission to go into our own depths with a little more courage so that we can also emerge with the truth we are seeking: OUR OWN.

keri smith

All my Life I wanted to Be an artist, but I was never quite sure what that would Look Like. I did not imagine any specifics, it was simply BE an ARTIST.

* ***

In 1993, my college roommate Elyse sent me "The Creative Companion", the first book by author and artist SARK. I began reading it the instant I pulled it out of the envelope and within an hour I knew what I wanted to do with my life. I wanted to be an artist and inspire the world to make their dreams real, just as SARK was doing for me.

A little over two years later, I started on that path – the path of being an artist, making a dream real and inspiring others to do the same. My goals were grand and my determination unstoppable, and I believed there was no reason why I couldn't do exactly what I wanted to do. The dream that I began that year was called Swirly.

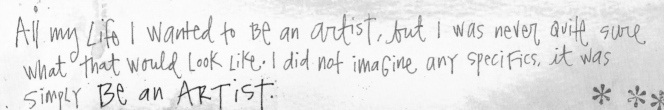

Future Swirly Girl

Swirly began in 1995 in a 10'x10' spare room in my apartment as a line of handmade greeting cards. Over the next six years, it grew to an internationally recognized brand with oodles of Swirly stationery and gift products, an inspirational gift book in three languages, fan mail, my own agent, an 1100 square foot office in downtown Santa Barbara and a ten pound portfolio. Swirly could be found in Target, Borders, Barnes & Noble, Michael's Craft Stores and well over 1000 other independent card and gift shops. In the spring of 2001, Swirly was going full steam ahead and I believed nothing would get in the way of it going as far as I wanted it to go, which meant Swirly displays at Target and an interview on the Oprah Winfrey show.

Something else happened in the Spring of 2001:
My Personal LIFE COMPLETELY COLLAPSED.

It is a long story, with words like divorce, cancer, heart attacks, brain tumors, death, broken homes, multiple moves and worlds of anger and heartache. At one point my friend and I were laughing at the fact that if I took the story I was currently living to a B-movie director whose films were only shown after midnight on cable TV, he or she would probably throw me out, saying my story was too unbelievable and outrageous.

There are some times in life when the only thing you can do to cope is to laugh. Believe it or not, I laughed a lot that year. Circumstances in my life had gotten so bizarre and heartbreaking I had no choice but to try to find humor in it.

By the end of that year my grand dreams for Swirly were replaced with longings of a different nature – a home of my own, miracle cancer cures and time with my friends and family. Suddenly, what I had been holding in my heart and mind for years and years – what I believed was my mission in the world – became rather unimportant and in some ways downright unattractive. I emerged from that year questioning *everything* and, surprisingly, feeling restricted by the Swirly persona I had created. I realized my work as an artist, a woman, a friend, a daughter, a partner and all the other roles that I played encompassed so much more, and in 2002 I found myself on a very different path than the one I was on just one year earlier. One with an entirely new set of priorities and a deeper understanding of my own self.

Although Swirly continues to encourage dreamers around the world to follow their hearts and will always be an important part of who I am, over the past many years I have slowly shed much of my Swirly skin. What has been revealed is much more authentic, albeit more vulnerable with very visible scars and flaws. As difficult as it has been, I have had to let go of the dream I carried with me for so much of my life in order to see all the greater possibilities that lay waiting for me beyond that world. Through the process, I realized living an authentic life was more important than building a commercially successful brand, and that while the two need not be mutually exclusive, it has become imperative that any work I do as an artist or otherwise keep those two in alignment.

What I learned from that tumultuous time is that success is not about profit and loss statements and fulfillment is not about product placement. "Life's Work" is not about fame or expertise and my proudest moments are much quieter than one might imagine. I learned that most dreams are not as unattainable as they might sometimes seem, but they rarely grant permanent feelings of security, contentment or immortality. Those feelings come from one place and one place only: within. Within our hearts, within our minds and within the moments we are able to be totally and completely present, drowning in appreciation for whatever that moment might be offering us. And this I also know to be unequivocally true: every moment, no matter how dire it may seem, has something to offer us. Every. Single. Moment.

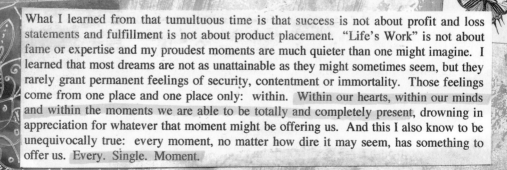

EVERY. SINGLE. MOMENT.

The pla_e where everything change_

safety

When everything you thought you wanted goes away and you have to rebuild your priorities and values from scratch, it can take some time to feel completely whole. I am still on a journey of self-discovery — perhaps always will be — and am beginning to find my way back to a part of myself I thought might be lost forever — that part of me that created a grand dream called SWIRLY and made that dream real.

It is as if this part of myself has been waiting quietly and patiently for me to notice her again, believe in her and return to her. Now that she knows I'm aware of her she is GLOWING brightly, yet still completely patient as I make my way towards her through the forest.

I am finding myself once again.

She is waiting with open arms.

MY desire to share The Things I Do in a way that expresses
their interconnectedness is not about wanting to put forth
an ideal, Glamorized version of my life. If anything,
I am trying to convey something more down to earth,
something that tells the story of an ordinary life filled with
the spectrum of ordinary human experiences, all tied
together by the desire to live a creative, meaningful life.

My day-to-day life is comprised of many things: I am an artist, a writer, a wife, a traveler, an
organizer, a runner, a cyclist and a philosopher. I am not especially confident in the kitchen, get
distracted easily, have bouts of overwhelming insecurity and love the smell of celery. In all of
these endeavors, mishaps and quirks, I strive to keep everything interconnected through integrity,
courage and compassion. No matter how ordinary, routine or habitual, I want my life to be driven
by these values.

This does not Guarantee Success or ease By any means, but there is incredible Freedom in my commitment to these core values. These Guideposts are always available no matter where I am or what I'm doing, and I don't have to spend time and enerGy trying to FiGure out HOW to maneuver my way through any situation.

My life is not about a specific joB description or title; it isn't aBout accomplishinG a Grand Goal that the rest OF the world deFines as success. It is aBout FollowinG my own path, expressinG mYSELF, trusting my Heart and sharing my journey. It is in aLL the little thinGs that the LarGer story is created, where meaninG is Given to every choice, every intention, every stroke oF the paint-Brush.

The story of a life is created when we Reach, Leap and TRY— sometimes succeeding, sometimes failing, sometimes learning our expectations far exceeded the reality of a wished-for experience, and sometimes VICE VERSA, where unbridled joy springs up in the most surprising places.

On a snowy January day in the Midwest I visited a cemetery, and came across a grave marker peeking through the snow. All that could be seen was a portion of the word **LOVED** in gold letters, a tiny piece of evidence of what lay beneath the expansive carpet of glittering snowflakes crunching beneath my feet. As I stood among the bare trees and inhaled deeply, I contemplated all the ways our lives become uniquely empty when a loved one passes on, how we create these testaments to make sure the world understands how deeply loved those closest to us were. It is this one particular piece of a person's life that most people want remembered above all else: that they were **LOVED**.

I imaGine there are very Few,
iF any, headstones that
read: SUCCESSFUL

RICH

FAMOUS

PERFECT.

There are many Endeavors we can
pursue in our Lives that provide a
Sense oF purpose and many positive attriButes
For which we can Be happily remembered,
But KnowinG the depth OF Love others
Feel For us has a waY OF makinG
all the other Facets oF our Lives
paLe in Comparison.

It is through the
love others feel for us
that our Real selves
are reflected, and
that is the joy we
will leave behind*
when our souls
move on to new
adventures.

* and also carry with us

In your quietest moments...
in those bare spaces where
the sound of your own breath
is all your ears register...

WHAT DOES YOUR HEART SAY TO YOU?

Follow its voice
to the Golden fields where your
very Best self is already

Soaring afore

the Landscape~

NOW

When we focus our energy towards constructing a passionate, meaningful life, we are tossing a pebble into the world, creating a beautiful ripple effect of inspiration. When one person follows a dream, tries something new or takes a daring leap, everyone nearby feels that energy, and before too long they are making their own daring leaps and inspiring yet another circle.

As this cycle continues, the world is lifted, and we are all encouraged to be that much more bold in the dreams we dream for ourselves.

We are taught to believe we will be
best served by getting things done
in a certain order:

1. Go to school
2. Get married
3. Have babies (or at least pets)
4. Have a career
5. retire
6. Enjoy Life

Lather
rinse
repeat

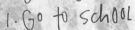LIFE, however, has a funny

way of throwing distractions, roadblocks
and other surprises our way, and

maneuvering through all of these things

often times makes sticking to a PLAN

rather difficult.

Our journey as Human Beings is not about Following a pre-ordained path, but about CREATING that path. Life rarely makes any more sense when things are done "in order". Life makes sense when we are centered in our Hearts and we let Go of resisting How our unique journey needs to unfold in its own Beautifully UNRULY WAY.

TIRUVANMIYUR PO <600041>
fgn-AIR-RPKT A ET41.1 IN
Counter No:1,OP-Code:AI
░░░░░░░░░░░░░░░░░░░░░░░░░░░░░░░░░░░
        INDIA POSTAGE
Amount:Rs122.00
░░░░░░░░░░░░░░░░░░░░░░░░░░░░░░░░░░░
22/04/2008   10:41
Wt:390grams To : USA, PIN:CA 90402

भारतीय डाक
INDIA POST

CUBA
HEX929

When the term "communication barrier" is uttered, it tends to conjure up an image of people from different countries, neither of whom can speak the other person's language. The truth is that these barriers exist no matter how well everyone understands each other's semantics, creating situations where spouses, siblings and best friends sometimes look at one another as if they were not just from different countries. But different galaxies altogether.

In any conversation, exchange or discussion, I try to imagine communication as a game of catch. I can either throw my words and ideas to the other person gently, in a way that enables them to accept what I am offering, or I can hurl something violently without thought or consideration. Do I want the other person to be able to receive and consider what I am trying to say or do I want the exchange to feel like I am throwing an object squarely at their forehead?

I Got hit in the Face By a Basketball with tremendous Force in the ninth Grade, and I still remember the shock of that experience. Communication has the potential to Feel the same way, where words can sideswipe our emotions and make us Feel completely thrown OFF Guard. Our words, and the way we deliver them, have tremendous power, particularly with those we are closest to. Choices must Be made every step of the way to keep the topic at hand in a space of common Ground; where intentions are centered around closeness and connection rather than being right.

Communicating From a healthy place takes effort and exercise just like anything else. Flexing our "Don't take things personally" muscle is a skill that requires commitment and discipline the same way training For a marathon does. We have to Be willing to do the work, Be present and take a deep Breath Before we Blurt out our First reactionary thought. Communication Barriers will always exist Between people. The Goal is not to avoid them or expect them to disappear. But to learn how to climb over and through them with our integrity - and relationships - intact.

It is innately Human to want to Hold on
to things — people, memories, objects, moments.
But life does not allow for such Grasping on
any permanent basis, and perhaps that is our
greatest challenge as expressive beings...
To create for the sake of creating.
knowing that what we create might not have
any value beyond our Doing it, knowing
it will someday be gone. To live for the
sake of living, knowing each moment we
have is over with every blink of an eye,
knowing we will someday be gone,

with only our creations left behind.

Cocoons and Pupæ   43

up at the leafless trees against the sky, and if you see a queer protuberance on a branch, or a spindle-shaped swelling, or a dead leaf rolled up and clinging to a twig, get at it if you can and investigate it.

The story of a caterpillar Going through a difficult, tender process in order to emerge in a more extraordinary form is an apt description of what we experience at different life stages as well as when the earth seems to crumble beneath us. Comparing our own process of change to something as exquisite as a butterfly enables us to focus on the beauty that can be attained within if we are willing to Go through our deepest internal mines, no matter how arduous. When a caterpillar transforms into a butterfly, it is losing its familiar form in order to become something entirely different, just as periods of loss and metamorphosis alter our own interior landscapes.

Through any period of change, there lies the opportunity to not only rebuild one's self and environment, but also demolish structures that have become outdated or destructive.

Where a caterpillar curls up into itself and does not re-surface until its entire being is transformed, as human beings with jobs, children and other responsibilities, we must do our morphing in the midst of day-to-day routines. This requires commitment, awareness and a clear sense of our deepest priorities. It requires effort when we might rather turn on the TV; it requires energy when we feel on the verge of collapsing. The work must be done to re-assemble the pieces of ourselves that have been shattered, otherwise we remain fractured individuals—not quite ourselves but not quite someone else either.

Life is nothing more than continuous cycles of transformation and growth. We become caterpillars, we go into the cocoon, we burst through as butterflies, and then we do it all over again. The belief that we are all gorgeous winged creatures waiting to emerge from our own experiences is a lovely one, but it is also important to embrace the cocoon, to cherish the times when we are deep in the act of change and shedding old selves. The in between times—which can sometimes be quiet and still and other times full of rage and ferocity—are where the real lessons are learned and where real change is possible.

The cocoon is where
we learn to slay
dragons, howl
at the moon and
embrace our flaws
more tenderly than
ever.

The cocoon is where
our souls do the
work they need to do,
where we are safe
enough to face the
truth with
eyes wide open.

Let your most authentic
Self be **SEEN**.

let by a mo
lf-hidden fro
the spri
whom t
very few
—Fair as a star,
Is shining in t

William

She lived unkno

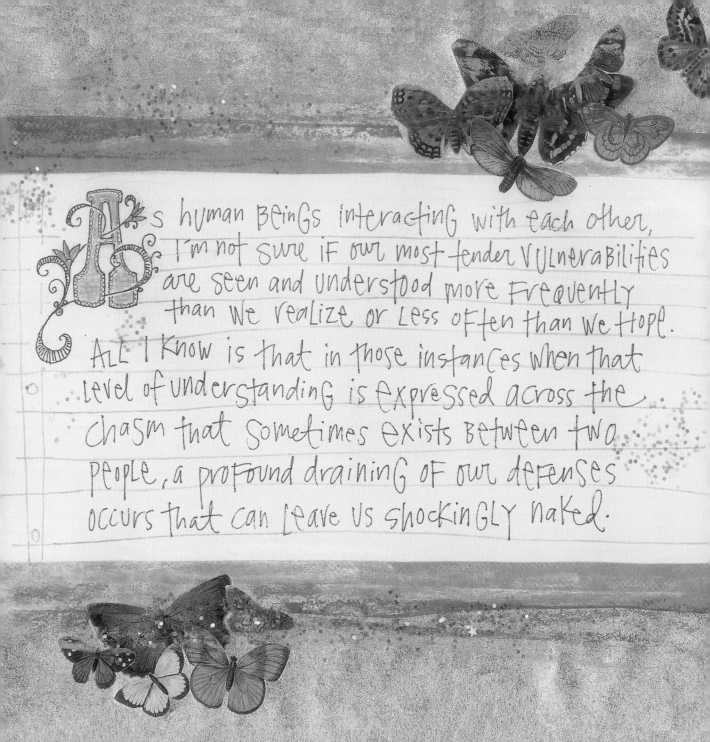

As human beings interacting with each other, I'm not sure if our most tender vulnerabilities are seen and understood more frequently than we realize or less often than we hope. All I know is that in those instances when that level of understanding is expressed across the chasm that sometimes exists between two people, a profound draining of our defenses occurs that can leave us shockingly naked.

As Frightening as this might Feel as we sit safely behind our armor of Fear, these interactions enable us to step out Fully into the sunlight, exposing parts of ourselves that are desperate for warmth, desperate for air; we believe our fears and vulnerabilities need to be Kept "safe" and hidden, locked away like something too precious for the elements, but in letting them be seen and maybe even held, we give them a chance to wander Freely, perhaps enough that we can eventually move forward with one less load to carry.

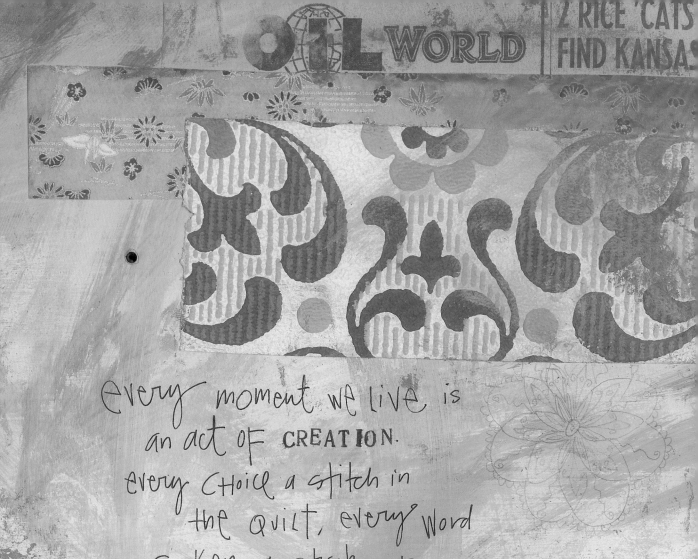

OIL WORLD

2 RICE 'CATS
FIND KANSAS

every moment we live is
an act of CREATION.
every choice a stitch in
the quilt, every word
spoken a stroke of
color on the canvas.

To create for the sake of creating

As an **ARTIST,** one of the experiences I love most is when someone asks what I do for a living and I get to answer, **"I AM AN ARTIST."** Whoever asks this question usually gets a dreamy look in their eyes and is immediately intrigued, whether it is one of my husband's investment industry colleagues or a twenty-something Japanese hipster on a flight to Tokyo.

After the "I am an Artist" cat is out of the bag, one of the following two comments ensues, almost without fail:

"I'm not creative at all."

"I can't even draw a stick figure!"

I find these comments humorous yet troubling. It is disheartening that so many people believe the only route to **BEING CREATIVE IS BY BEING A PROFESSIONAL ARTIST.** the conclusion being that if you are anything but an artist, you must not be creative.

At all.

So many people have absorbed this as an indisputable fact, and will even go so far as to argue the point with me, insisting they do not have a creative cell in their body. They believe I have been blessed by some kind of magic DNA that is given out sparingly throughout the human race.

This is astounding to me when I think about the number of colors that are now in the jumbo box of crayola crayons*, how crayola has been in the coloring business since 1885 and now boasts a product line that includes markers, pencils, chalk, clay and glitter. That business would not be so thriving if there weren't hoards of children wanting to make a creative mess for one simple reason: because it's fun.

How did we get from devouring 120 sticks of color to "I'm not creative at all?"

*120

Being creative feeds a well that, as humans, we are all born with. To watch the level of abandonment with which children create and not recognize this deep need within ourselves is a bit like trying to stay cold in front of a roaring fire.

We can't help but want to create.*

We are human, after all.

*and we ALL have unique creative gifts.

7
6
5
4
3
2
1

Your
*
Best
Friend

next-d
*
neighB

parents
*

5   3   1   1   2   3   4   5   6   7   9

*
society

1

*

Your
*
hero

4

Find Your true center.
| 24 | 25 | 26 | 27 | 28 | 29 | 30 | 31 | 32 | 33 | 34 | 35 |

6

7

Your
2nd Grade
*
teacher

*
media

8

*

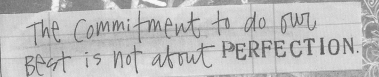

The Commitment to do our Best is not about PERFECTION.

Doing our Best is about offering what we can Give with the highest Level of integrity and most sincere intention. It is about Knowing in our Hearts we have made every effort we were able to make in any Given situation.

Sometimes the Greatest effort we can make appears small. It matters not as much whether our endeavors Live up to someone else's standards but how confidently we can say we stayed true to our own.

When we do our best, it is inevitable:
WE FLOURISH.

A quick glimpse of my 40th birthday party would have shown me giving it my all on the dance floor we created in our living room, disco ball and all. Had you been able to take a peek at what was going on in my brain, you would have seen me on the verge of tremendous disappointment that the dance floor I worked so hard to create wasn't packed with all of my friends.

It was a small piece of time during an otherwise perfect evening, but what was so fascinating in those few moments was how aware I was of the fact that my expectations were on the cusp of making me totally bummed out. By all appearances, I was the happiest woman in the world, but inside I was having to talk myself through my bubbling disappointment.

In the weeks leading up to the party, particularly as I discussed song lists with the DJ I had splurged on for the event, I focused on an image of our home as Studio 54, with the Bee Gees spilling out the windows and floating across our lawn as all of my friends and I got funky inside. That was the scene that kept repeating in my mind anytime I talked about the party, over and over again.

When the party was in full swing, the dance floor was fairly sparse, and over the course of the evening I managed to cajole everyone out there at one point in time or another, but never all at once. When it became apparent my perfect disco party wasn't going to materialize, I had to work through it immediately by making one simple choice:

stay attached to my expectations and let my disappointment rule the night, or let it go and just have fun.

I did choose the latter, and will always look back at this night as a huge success. Not only because everyone there, especially me, had a great time, but also because I learned a valuable lesson about keeping my expectations in check. It was a small, inconsequential event, but when the stakes are low, we have the opportunity to practice positive habits gently. These "less important" experiences can provide a foundation and give us a point of reference when faced with similar struggles in the future.

Situations, events and even disco parties are all going to unfold however they are going to unfold, no matter what grand plans or visions we might have been holding onto up until that point. There is definitely room in the world for each of us to make a dream real as long as there is also space available to let the dream give each of us its own surprising twists and turns.

No one had a clue Christine was struggling to overcome her expectations as she rocked out to Def Leppard with Blair…

Quilting. Plan mo...
...ly placed. Stamp ...
...ing. Lay waddi...
...ith motif up. Stit...
...with sharp-point...
...adding outside stitc...
...ce wrong side to cover...

self

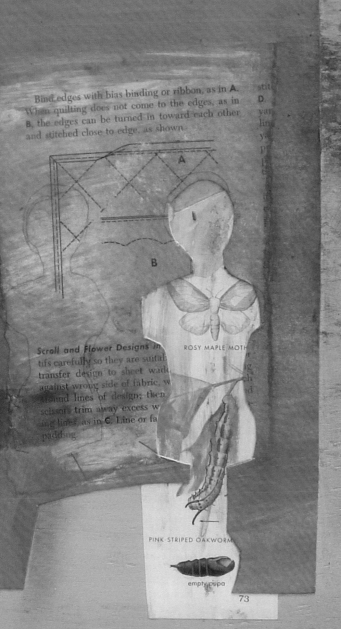

Bind edges with bias binding or ribbon, as in **A**. When quilting does not come to the edges, as in **B**, the edges can be turned in toward each other and stitched close to edge, as shown.

stit...
D.
ya...
lin...
y...
p...
pl...

Scroll and Flower Designs in...
tifs carefully so they are suitab...
transfer design to sheet wad...
against wrong side of fabric, w...
around lines of design; then...
scissors trim away excess w...
ing lines, as in **C**. Line or fa...
padding...

ROSY MAPLE MOTH

PINK-STRIPED OAKWORM

empty pupa

73

discovery

ETABLISSEMENTS ALLEZ FRÈRES

BOUGIE DE LUXE

TRIPLE PRESSION

PARIS 1, Rue St Martin, 1, PARIS

13º PISO

of needs, the desire to delight a loved one—all

As I enter my fourth decade, distanced enough from the most challenging period of my life to fully appreciate all of its deeper beauty and transformative gifts, I find myself feeling the tiniest bit WISE.

Not wise in an ALL-KNOWING, I-have-it-all-figured-out kind of way, but wise in the sense that I've grown comfortably enough in my own skin to examine what this word means to me within the context of THE STORY MY LIFE IS CREATING.

wis·dom (wĭz′dəm) n. 1. Insightful understanding of what is true, right, or enduring. 2. Native good judgment <had the wisdom to leave well enough alone> 3. The amassed learning of philosophers, scientists, and scholars.
wisdom tooth n. The last tooth on each side of both jaws in humans.
wise¹ (wīz) adj. wis·er, wis·est. 1. Having great learning. 2. Having discernment : sagacious. 3. Sensible : prudent. 4. a. Having awareness or information : knowing. b. Cunning : shrewd. 5. Slang. Offensively bold or impudent. —wise′ly adv.
wise² (wīz) n. Manner or fashion <in this wise>
-wise suff. 1. In a given way, direction, or position <counterclockwise> 2. Informal. Regarding <dollarwise>
wise·a·cre (wīz′ā′kər) n. Informal. One who pretends to be learned or clever.
wise·crack (wīz′krăk′) n. Slang. A witty or facetious remark. —wise′crack′ v.
wish (wĭsh) n. 1. A desire or longing for something. 2. An expression of a wish <Make a wish.> 3. Something desired. —v. 1. To desire or long for : want. 2. To make or express a wish for <wished us a safe trip> 3. To bid <wish someone good night> 4. To request or command <I wish you to go at once.> 5. To force or impose upon another. —wish′er n.

I believe wisdom is having an awareness of all the questions we can explore in any given situation.

I believe it is becoming more at ease with not having absolute answers.

I believe it is about choosing to live with integrity even when no one is watching, about living by my highest standards regardless of the choices those around me make.

I believe wisdom is about accepting that life is difficult but recognizing the beauty that exists on this very bumpy journey.

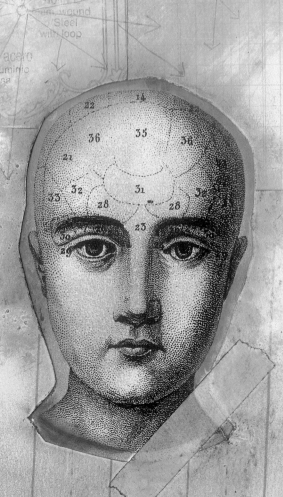

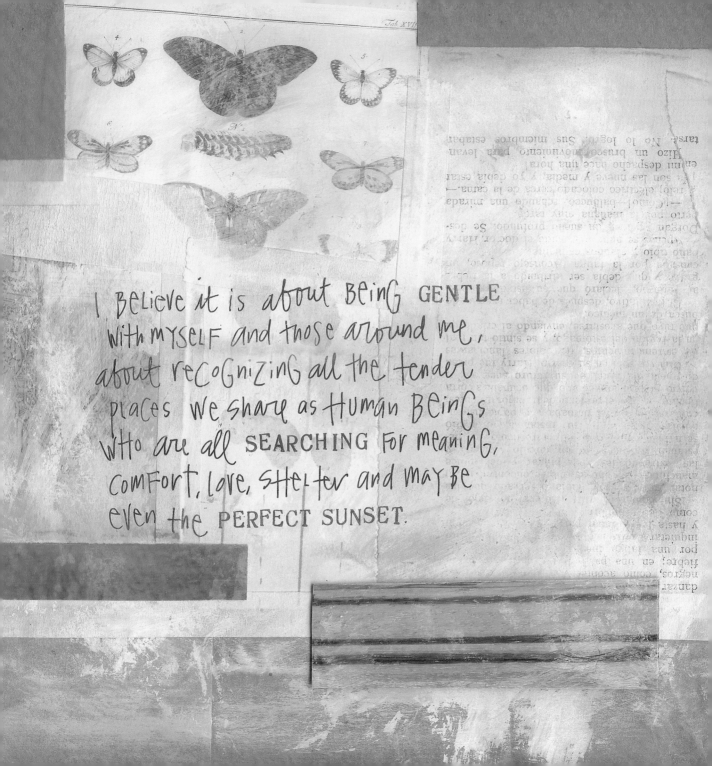

I believe it is about being GENTLE
with myself and those around me,
about recognizing all the tender
places we share as Human Beings
who are all SEARCHING for meaning,
comfort, love, shelter and may be
even the PERFECT SUNSET.

It is about Getting Lost in the Journey of my Questions rather than insisting on always BEING RIGHT.

It is about draining the tension out of my Heart, mind and BODY during periods of uncertainty and appreciating that such experiences are more about Wide Open Possibility than impending DOOM.

The more I ACCEPT that my most profound Questions are ultimately unknowable, the Less emphasis I place on perfection, certainty and security, the wiser I Feel.

As MY mind Quiets down and I watch the Bare Branches
dance outside MY Window, MY Heart SWELLS,
and the tiny Bud OF Wisdom inside me Begins to open
up, petal BY petal. It is nourished not BY Needing
to KNOW but BY Wanting to EXPLORE, BY Being
Willing to WANDER as I ponder the extraordinary

MYSTERY OF LIFE.

REFUGE building
HOME
dwelling
residence house retreat
NEST
Shelter COTTAGE
haven

대한민국 우표
묘작도
30
REPUBLIC OF KOREA

भारत INDIA
50

CUBA 1976
correos
50
PAISAJE CUBANO FEDERICO F. CAVADA

What does it
mean to you?

home (hōm) n. 1. a. A place where one lives: residence. b. An apartment or house. 2. A household. 3. A place of origin. 4. A habitat, as of an animal or plant. 5. The goal in a game, as baseball. 6. An institution for those who need help or care. *syns: ABODE, DIGS, DWELLING, HABITATION, HOUSE, LODGINGS, PAD, PLACE —adv. 1. At or toward home. 2. At the center of a target. 3. To the heart or center. —v. homed, homing. 1. To return home. 2. To be guided to a target electronically. —homeless adj.

LOT NO.
I 07296
117
BEKINS
VAN LINES CO.

LOT NO.
I 07296
106
BEKINS
VAN LINES CO.

LOT NO.
I 07296
121
BEKINS
VAN LINES CO.

LOT NO.
I 07296
060
BEKINS
VAN LINES CO.

STANWIX SQ 700
ETHAN ALLEN LA 4600

Norman, OK 1
Quantico, VA 12
Norfolk, VA 1
33 Jacksonville, NC 1
34 Alexandria, VA 1 2 3 4 5
35 Blacksburg, VA 1 2 3 4
36 Athens, GA 1 2 3 4
37 Columbia, MO 1
38 Santa Barbara, CA 1 2 3 4 5 6 7
39 Solvang, CA 1
40 Los Angeles, CA 1 2 3 4 5

When I think of the word family, a number of different thoughts and emotions spring forth which send me into an instant whirlwind of ideas, images, desires, fears and dreams. This sounds more tumultuous than it really is, as I have thus far never developed a concrete idea of what family means, so I have learned to live in a state of mild confusion about the subject.

In many ways, a family is a creative act just like anything else. There must be a commitment to whatever ideal we envision for ourselves and then the work must be done to make it a reality. This can mean any number of different things, from getting married to forgiveness. If creating a family is a priority, then choices must be made to support that, which is very often easier said than done.

In a world full of so much uncertainty, family is something we all want to be able to rely on no matter what. Despite this deep human yearning, it is rare to meet someone who has a completely stable family with no baggage, anger, deep regret or painful scars. The truth is that families are complicated entities made up of HUMAN BEINGS, and as individuals we are all trying to make our way in the world in our own way. Sometimes the journeys we want to take collide with others, including family members, and this is when conflict can arise. At some point in time or another, our notions of family will very likely be challenged.

Whatever we might have been taught to believe about family growing up will someday come into question, and that is when we must develop our own definition and sense of family. ☞ This is perhaps one of the most profound turning points we all experience — that of shedding ideals put upon us by parents or society and creating our own. These might not even be that different from what we've carried with us so far, but the act of making them uniquely our own, however that looks, is what enables us to find peace in whatever our definition of family is.

My life experiences have shaped the way I define family, so in that sense my definition is like no other. Different life paths lead to different definitions and ideas of many things, from family to success.

I have come to accept the Fact that family, for me, is not a static, permanent thing, but a TRIBE of people I love that contracts and expands in different circumstances. I have Learned to TRUST that I will always have the support I need even if my support system does not fit the "normal" definition of family.

I Believe I will always have the family I need... the family I have created.

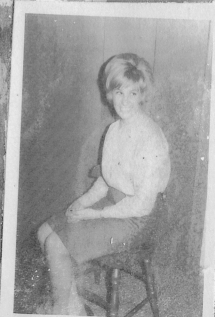

MONTGOMERY,
CORSICANA, TEXAS

Merle
Evelyne
Robert
Doris
Dorothy
Geneva
Christine
Waleta
Joseph
Mattie
Harry
Sadie
John
Maggie
Opal
Jewel
Rose
Frank
Bessie
Nell
Ernestine
Alvin
Patricia
Ruth
Walter
Lois
Suzanne

It is astounding How Little
it takes to make me Feel

DEEPLY HAPPY...

* the Sound OF rain Falling outside my window.
* a Long, hot Shower after a day Working
    in my studio
* the smell OF jasmine By moonLiGht
* the memory OF my Grandma's hands, and
    the way they Felt in mine
* staying up Late,
    when the world
    outside is still
* sLeeping in the
    Next day

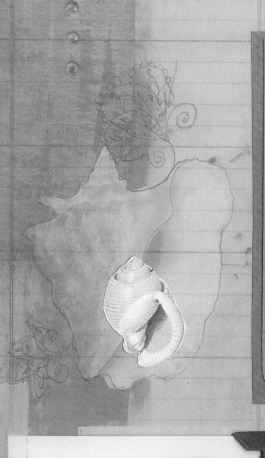

Grand moments are nice, but it is the smaller Gems that create the most exquisite beauty, the tiny jewels that adorn our lives every single day.

Lovely to meet you today, Coco - keep shining BRIGHT! Susannah xo.

All I was doing was washing dishes, on an evening like every other evening that week where my husband and I met each other at our kitchen table later than usual for dinner, both exhausted from running around like lunatics all day. It being December, he was dealing with a huge end of the year to do list at work and I was playing my annual role as Santa Claus, in charge of all things Christmas. We had a simple meal and I was cleaning up as he sat at his laptop hunting for gifts, when I looked over at him and suddenly felt a gentle wave of contentment melt into me like a drop of honey in hot tea. It was as if there was a force in the world that wanted to make sure I recognized how precious that moment was, and in that strangely poetic instance, I saw it with perfect clarity: **this is it.**

This is the life we have worked so hard to create.

These are the moments we Get to enjoy...Quiet nights at home, when we share our days with each other, eat a home-cooked meal, read a book and Later, fall asleep next to each other in a cozy bed and perfect silence.

this is our consummate joy.

As much as Life's extraordinary moments are powerful in their own way, I often find the quieter ones more meaningful, more lovely in their simplicity. I am the only person in the world who Gets to create and share a Home with my Husband, with all the tiny details that entails. It is within those specifics that the simple becomes the divine, the "normal" becomes wholly unique.

That evening — for no reason in particular — was its own tiny universe, an instant that encompassed every other instant of my wonderfully imperfect Life... and I held it like a fragile, dainty butterfly that wanted nothing more than for me to stop and notice it.

Then in one quick instant,
it Fluttered away.

and Before I could BLINK,

it was Gone.

CREATIVITY

is Not

about

Perfection...

it is about being

WILd, Silly,

and DOWNright

OutraGeous.

"HOW DID YOU LEARN HOW TO DO IT?"

...is the question I usually get in any discussion about my greeting card business, and my answer is always the same: by doing everything wrong the first time.

From figuring out how to create a purchase order form to arranging images for my printer, that was my modus operandi, and while I did not set out to learn everything I needed to know by making mistakes, I must admit it was a very effective learning tool.

½ 1 2 3 4 5 6 7 8 9 10 11 12 13 14

After four decades of amassing heaps of mistakes professionally and otherwise, I have developed a very specific philosophy about them, the key point being that mistakes do not equal failure.

Mistakes are simply human.

They can result when trying something new, taking steps toward a dream, interacting with our friends as well as when cooking, driving and even spelling. Mistakes are part of life, and without them our journey would be a lot less interesting.

Even when we do our best, it is always well within the realm of possibility that we will make mistakes. Knowing this, we can either choose to live in fear of them, or accept that they just might happen and in such an event the best thing we can do is take responsibility for them. Trying to run away from them only forces us to expend that much more energy dealing with them; to simply stand up and say, "I made a mistake," immediately frees us from unnecessary baggage. We might have to take time to rectify our mistakes, but that is at least forward movement and positive action. Attempts made towards covering up, shifting blame or avoiding responsibility have a way of pulling us down in the muck, unable to move beyond whatever error occurred.

In doing just about everything incorrectly the First time I tried anything as I built Swirly, I felt very clumsy and inept. Looking Back, it is easy to see that my mistakes were the result of inexperience more than anything else. Beyond those details, it was that journey of many tiny missteps that helped me learn how to maneuver my way through all the Fumbles I continue to make from a place of confidence, grace and integrity. I learned over and over again that my mistakes did not take away from the truth that I was smart, capable, creative or doing my best — they only meant that I wasn't infallible.

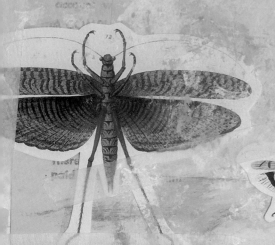

In all of our unique slips and stumbles, we learn about ourselves and we grow.

We find the way to hold our head high in' our imperfections and have confidence in ourselves through our blunders.

We discover it is possible to SOAR even if we've tripped, bumped, teetered, or tottered, that sometimes losing our footing enables us to take greater leaps than we thought possible.

I believe it is possible for every element of my life to interconnect in a way that makes it feel less like a pressure-filled balancing act and more like an extraordinary, creative

EXPERIMENT

where every act, no matter how mundane, is a piece of the puzzle that creates my very best life.

yes. Insert slide fastener at closing.
e procedure as for slip-cover. Over
fabric and tape of slide fastener together

السلامة العالمية المشمعة
شط عار
SAFETY MATCHES
واربد احمد جيب شمسان عدن

Egypt

2.º **PISO**
5

1930年代初期、パリ・ラファイエット系百貨店として〈高級品〉を印象づけていくか
〈大衆品〉を印象づけていくかにより、各百貨店の商品構成と売場面積に〈大きな

We all have people in our lives who we want to impress, who we hope will like us, who we want to make proud. In any relationship, the important thing to remember is that this kind of respect should not be given away haphazardly. Your deepest devotion should be granted to those who like you, are impressed by you and proud of you **BECAUSE YOU'RE YOU.**

You will find your way to like-minded souls by **BEING YOURSELF** and creating a life according to your values. The more you try to squeeze yourself into someone else's mold, the more contentment will drain from your spirit.

✳ ✳ ✳ ✳ ✳ ✳

I tried desperately to squeeze myself into a teeny tiny box for someone else for a very long time. This box represented the amount of room this person had in his heart for an authentic relationship with me. He was interested in a relationship with me **IF AND ONLY IF** our interactions were exclusively on his terms and according to his ideas of who I ought to be and how I ought to behave.

I ALLOWED THIS FOR MANY YEARS.

Then one day I had no choice but to break out of the BOX, and the instant I did this he became unbearably cruel, accusing me of being all the things I strive NOT to be - selfish, ungrateful, foolish, without integrity.

It took a while, but I finally realized the absolute truth of this situation — that whatever this person's opinion of me was, it need not have ANY impact on me, because this person DID NOT KNOW ME AT ALL.

Our "relationship" had been built around the fact that I existed in the TINY BOX, so whatever he (thought) he knew about me, or chose to believe about me, was based on interactions in which I never authentically shared myself. I shared only as much as what could fit in the BOX, and the rest I kept hidden.

What he experienced was a shadow of me, self-perpetuated by my desire to earn his love. I literally blocked my own sunlight, and this seemed to please him. I gave him this power for a LONG time.

Once I unchained myself from this relationship, all the control I had offered him unquestioningly returned to me, and I learned how to soar like never before. As painful as facing the truth of our dynamic was, it gave me the strength to stand firm in my own integrity and rooted in my own self.

****

Letting go of these relationships, as healthy as this might be in the long run, can still cause a unique kind of grief, but in the destruction and dismantling, new space opens up for your most authentic self to emerge. You deserve to move through this world committed to your own ideals and strongest sense of self, and there are people the world over who want nothing more from you than to see your wings spread wide, glimmering across a

PERFECT BLUE SKY.

"Life has taught me that it is filled with unbelievable beauty, limitless opportunities and untold miracles.

"One must take the time to understand it, to appreciate it and to live it. Just think, all of a sudden, when you wake up each morning, life isn't life — IT'S LIFE! it is beyond belief."

At any given moment You Have the Power to say:

THIS
IS
NOT
HOW
THE
STORY
IS
GOING
TO
END.

FULLY

Living a Life ↓ committed to one's strongest values is not a way of life for the meek, the fearful or the squeamish. It is a way of life that I sometimes curse myself for choosing, especially in those moments when the allure of wallowing and giving up shines brightly in my peripheral vision, wanting to pull me in like a moth to a flame. Those are the moments when I want to be lazy and take whatever is the easiest way out and run the greatest risk of losing my way.

It is in these experiences when I must DIG deep and stay FOCUSED on BEING the Kind OF person I strive to BE.

It is easy to be a compassionate person with those who are kind to you,

more challenging with those who have hurt or abandoned you.

It is in those moments when the Standards we set For ourselves are truly tested, and iF we are able to WALK through them with our inteGrity infact, we have SUCCeeded in the most proFound way we are CAPABLE oF SUCCeedinG as Human BeinGs in a COMPLiCated WORLd.

DREAM

BELIEVE

GROW

WANDER

HOPE

FLY

farther

THIS is the Moment that Matters... All moments Before and After are

DREAMS.

In any relationship, many problems—maybe even ALL—are not based on anything REAL, but are instead created and nurtured by a laundry list of fears. Fears we carry with us and fears that others in our vicinity throw into the mix. It is as if we all agree to believe the myth that we exist in dark rooms apart from one another, but the truth is that we are TOGETHER in a wide open field where we can all have what we desire, and the desires we each LONG for are the same:

* We want to be close.

* We want to feel safe.

* We want to be connected.

* And we are afraid.

We will very Likely always have to wrestle with our unique mixed BAG OF Fears. From time to time they may interrupt the otherwise pleasant Back and Forth volley of dreams, thoughts & emotions we have with those we Love and Care about.

As much as it is possiBle, we need to have Compassion For those Fears rather than disdain, to reCoGniZe that they are soft spots in our Hearts rather than walls around them. They are spaces that have TREMENDOUS CAPACITY FOR GROWTH.

BeCause iF we can HeLp one another move Beyond these Fears and replace them with Greater Levels OF trust, we can move to a truly sacred existence where Love is the GuidinG Force.

[For TaYLor]

every single moment you are writing the story of your life.

In an age when the phenomenal success and generosity of Oprah Winfrey stands as the shining example of what it means to BE **inspiring**, it is easy to fall into the trap of thinking our choices and actions won't make a difference, let alone be counted as "inspirational." But inspiration exists everywhere, in **everything** we do from the moment we wake up to the instant we fall asleep. In the midst of meals, errands, work and play, what we do has an impact on Humanity.

We are all making our way through a complicated society that is filled with distractions, frustrations and injustice. We are all on a quest for meaning, trekking through our own internal jungles to find the answers we seek. As we weave the tapestry of our own lives, we are each capable of acting as a beacon, as inspirational beings who others look to for guidance, joy and wisdom.

We each inspire, delight
and contribute to the world
by creating a cozy home,
showing kindness to a stranger,
writing a poem, laughing out loud,
saying No, saying Yes,
saying I'm sorry, saying I love you.

All of these gestures and countless others
emit a **radiant light**, and the
world needs as much light as possible.

Light from every smile,
every gentle word,
every daring leap.

給　料
（給料明細書在中）

月分

所属

殿

ready to transform,

When you are standing at the bottom of a mountain that you have no choice but to climb, taking one day at a time is the only thing that matters. It is the only way you will reach the top of that mountain, the

only way you will find your way through the darkness. **IT IS SOLID.**

It is reliable. It is like the rising of the sun everyday— it is something you might not take much time to notice, but it is always there, a reminder that each new day holds endless possibility.

LEGS टांगें

FEET पैर

I travel to learn about the world, to
smell the aromas of a strange city and drink
the colors of a foreign land; I travel to
meet friends that are now living their lives
on another part of the planet, totally
unaware of the fact that we will someday
find our way to each other;

I travel for all of these reasons
and more, but beyond all the
joy I experience when I embark
to a new spot on the world atlas,
I travel to discover myself, as
that terrain is sometimes the
strangest and most unfamiliar
of all...

OH how I have **failed!** In relationships, in Business, in Freshman Chemistry at Virginia Tech. In a multitude of places, **i have failed.**

And I have Failed For one simple reason: Because I've **tried.**

In any effort, Failure is a possibility.

And Beyond any Failure, there is always Room to **try again.**

SIERRA DE LOS ORGANOS

I do not wish for an EASY LIFE.* I do not walk this earth imagining how much better my life could be if only THIS or if only THAT. I have dreams I want to pursue, goals I want to accomplish and experiences I want to enjoy, but beyond any wanting, imagining and hoping I also nurture a quiet space in my life for ACCEPTANCE. A space where I can lean deeper into whatever might feel less than ideal and explore whether or not my initial judgments were accurate. Often times what I thought might be a source of unending woe turns out to be an

incredible blessing.

* This feels rather silly to say because compared to most I have an incredibly easy life.

How often do we spend time and energy searching for, trying to find or hoping to construct some image of "PERFECT", some definition we have decided is the only way we can possibly find contentment?

How many gifts and treasures are overlooked because our attention is so fiercely focused on what is not available?

When I wake up each day, I do not set out to create an existence of "perfect." I instead try to open myself up as much as possible to all the perfect moments that exist in an imperfect life.

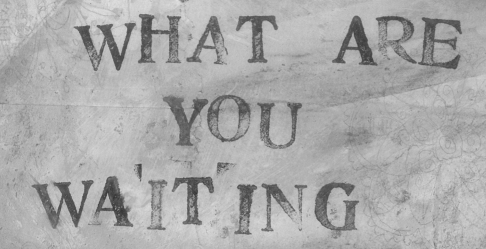

WHAT ARE YOU WAITING FOR?

Soon after my husband and I got settled into our new home in Los Angeles, we had friends over for dinner who gave us a bottle of Dom Perignon champagne as a housewarming gift. This was a very special treat, and we immediately put the bottle in our refrigerator, deciding we would save it for a special occasion.

Many months later, with the bottle still waiting for that "perfect moment" to be uncorked, we found ourselves cooking a roasted chicken on a quiet Sunday evening. Out of the blue, my husband brought out the bottle and decided that would be the night we enjoyed it. So our "special occasion" turned out to be nothing more than a simple dinner for two in our own cozy living room. We opened the champagne, it was delightful, and I now look at that evening as a special occasion for no reason other than we decided to make it one. We could have continued to wait for some other evening with special significance and used that as an excuse to open the champagne, but instead we opened the champagne on what looked like an average evening, and suddenly that average evening became extraordinary.

There are so many circumstances, situations, ideas and dreams that make us believe we have to wait for the PERFECT TIME. From buying a house and having children to starting a business or trying a new hobby, there is the notion that everything will be easier if we wait... and wait... until all areas of our lives are in perfect alignment.

While it makes sense to have certain things in order before new mountains are conquered, it is all too easy to fall into a pattern of seeing **A DREAM** as something that can only be realized LATER:

"When I have a bigger studio."

"When I have more money in the bank."

"When all my laundry is done."

I have learned that instead of waiting for the perfect time to do something, the time I happen to do something turns out to be perfect for its own reasons, reasons I could not have imagined before I began. Waiting for the right timing can be a positive, productive strategy, but at some point a conscious choice must be made to follow a dream or an idea – or even just a quiet evening enjoying a bottle of pricey champagne – and take the first step towards making it real.

Then suddenly that first step is transformed into the sparkling jewel that is longed for by so many people in so many situations – the PERFECT TIME.

Your wings already exist.
All you have to do is
Be willing to
Spread them
open.

The world wants
to see them.

MY First visit to Tokyo was not about seeing specific landmarks and marking them off a tour Guide checklist. It was about observing a new city with its own unique traits, quirks and norms that are far different from my own in the United States. It was about leaving my hotel room and entering an entirely different environment and not wanting to stick out like an obnoxious, disrespectful sore thumb. Each situation I encountered — a meal, shopping, navigating the subway system, taking a taxi — gave me an opportunity to be still, observe, and follow what the locals did. Each day was an exercise in releasing assumptions that my way of doing things was best or even appropriate and opening myself up to something I had not yet considered or experienced.

In Tokyo, there is a particular way you give a salesperson your credit card (with both hands, placing it on a small tray), there is a particular way whatever you buy is packaged (very neatly, very securely, even a washcloth). There is a specific way boxes are wrapped, a pattern of haphazard-looking folds where only one piece of tape is needed to hold it all together.

All of these details I noticed and learned by allowing myself the time to absorb my surroundings slowly rather than plowing through the day trying to cram in as many activities and sights as possible.

I went to Tokyo thinking I would feel lost, disconnected and disoriented. Instead, I felt oddly at home. I appreciated the gracefulness of the people, the attention to detail and the peculiar way the city felt quiet despite all the cars and people. Most everyone was quite reserved, but I found myself practically stalking a group of teenage girls one afternoon, giggling at how clearly I saw my own my own teenage self in them, full of high pitched squeals of nervous laughter with Hello Kitty paraphernalia dangling from purses, necklaces and keychains, clinking and jingling everywhere they went. I imagined them in school, staring at the boys they thought were the cutest, and gathering together like this each day to swoon and dream over milkshakes and metallic pink cell phones. Are we, as human beings, really so different from each other? Sometimes yes, many times, not so much.

YUZEN

ORIGAMI

ありがとうございまし
お待ちしております
お客

I realize I only saw one small layer of life in Tokyo, and as a 5'7" Blonde, I was viewed and treated by everyone I came into contact with as an obvious foreigner. This was not bad, but it was no doubt different from how they interact with friends & family. I don't believe I gained any special insight into Japanese life or Tokyo's social norms. As is true of all of my travel experiences, what I learned most about was myself - my ability to adapt, my passion for the simple act of walking in an unfamiliar neighborhood and watching an old woman ride her bike through a cemetary with a basket of flowers, my cultural biases, my fears, and all the other things I carry with me, as I wander on my own in a new city that speaks a strange language. As I meander here and there, I am alone with my thoughts. It is in this particular kind of alone-ness that I sometimes make startling discoveries - about the world and my self.

I do not travel to follow itineraries.

I travel to see whatever I happen to see.

I travel to challenge myself, to step outside of myself and hopefully return home slightly changed, maybe even slightly wiser.

All it takes is a willingness to wander, to make mistakes, to ask for help, to observe, to follow my instincts,

to face fears and step outside my comfort zone.

This is true when I travel to a new place and in so many other situations — when I begin a work of art, when I argue with my husband.

It is true no matter what, every single day, wherever I happen to be.

Life can be adorned with many wonderful experiences, accomplishments and even MATERIAL OBJECTS, but the deepest joy exists in those rare instances of CLARITY, when there is no WANTING, no YEARNING, no CLINGING to any idealized life we BELIEVE exists somewhere other than EXACTLY where we are.

RAT DE POCHE

EXTRA BUTTONS

Many years ago, in the midst of one of the most challenging episodes of my life, a dear friend said seven small words to me:

"ALL YOU HAVE TO DO IS RECEIVE."

The very instant those words were punctuated
with a tiny period, they became embedded in my
psyche, and I have since carried them with
me everywhere I go, passing them out like
Daisies in quiet conversations over coffee
and broken hearts.

Whenever I share those words with someone,
regardless of the circumstances, the reaction
to this truth is curiously consistent:
there is an almost imperceptible pause,
followed by a nod that is slightly reticent
and painfully tender. It is a moment when I
am able to observe the unveiling of another
person's vulnerability, when seven little
words act as links in a chain that pulls
even the toughest defenses down, if only
for a moment.

To receive is something many seem to struggle with, very often over concerns that someone else's giving will deplete them of some all-important item:

* time
* energy
* money
* love

Being told it is OK to receive freely and without guilt touches the most delicate place in our hearts, for when we are given permission to receive we are being told something else as well, something even more important: that we are worthy and deserving of all the love and support we need.

There are times in life when we are called upon to give, and times when the world needs us to receive. We must offer ourselves in both arenas, knowing they each feed and inspire the world. We give. We take. We ask, we receive, and in all of these exchanges, we contribute.

We would all prefer to experience as little emotional pain and Heartache, as possible but must be discerning in our Quest to steer clear of any potential despair. If not kept at Bay, Fear can quietly close our Hearts to the extraordinary Bliss that can be Had if we are willing to love **WITH ABANDON.**

The more we aspire to avoid pain, the more we lose sight of all the joy

SURRENDER

Has to offer.

How divine is one's inner Garden 🦋 when Full of twisted and tangled vines Sprouting Blossoms of all colors, shapes and sizes... I speak of friendship, particularly the Friendships I share with my GIRLFRIENDS.

So much has been said of the powerful connections between women throughout history –

how can I possibly add anything new?

But I must try, For the women in my Life have made me who I am, and it is the women in my Life who I count on more than anyone to help me Get through whatever Life decides to throw my way.

It is not that I do not rely on my husband or that my friendships take anything away from my marriage. It is more that without one, the other suffers greatly, and without both in my life, I would be woefully out of balance. If my husband is my heart and the largest recipient of my energy, attention, devotion, passion and commitment, then my girlfriends are the veins, pumping this energy throughout all areas of my life and *keeping me alive*. I think my husband ought to write individual thank you notes to all of my female tribe members, for without them he would have a much harder time with me.

I look at the women in my Life and see how they have made me a Better person in very specific ways, how they have inspired me to take Bolder Leaps, try more daring Feats and Laugh that much Louder along the way.

After living on this earth for more than three decades in **33** different homes, I have created a circle of friends that, despite being scattered here and there, is a circle I know I can count on unequivocally.

They are the ones who will carry me through my greatest sorrows and most spectacular triumphs by doing one small yet profound thing: *being there.*

Being present.

Sitting still with my pain.

Allowing a quiet moment to exist when the world around us is in hysterics.

Sharing their dreams and exposing their fears.

Accepting me as I am while at the same time encouarging me to be a better person.

Holding a sacred space for my victories.

I need my girlfriends like I need to breathe— it is something I cannot imagine my life being without. My marriage thrives when I feel the strength of my female tribe behind me and I trust everything and everyone more easily when I look at my circle of friends. What could possibly go wrong in my life when I have these beauties supporting me?

How bad can things be when these women - who could choose to rely on anyone in the world to support them - choose to rely on me? A burden I happily accept...a burden that is not at all a burden, but the sweetest of all responsibilities. To return the favor of a deep and luscious friendship - to give back what I have received.

Being an ARTiST is something I have Been doing From the time I could WALK, and what I always dreamed For MYSELF Growing up. I consider it a tremendous Honor to Be able to say "I am an artist", and I still say it with a slightly stunned tingling in my Heart. Part oF me doesn't Feel Like it is REAL, and another part oF sometimes doesn't Feel Like I deserve it. me

But it is WHo I AM and WHAT I DO and I have Learned to create my own DeFinition oF what it means to BE AN ARTIST.

It is tempting to insert the word "SUCCessFul" BeFore "Artist" in that sentence, But these two words Feel redundant when reFerring to my own LiFe. I AM AN ARTIST, and Being able to say this is my Greatest achievement.

It is just that simple.

So there you have it: my greatest success story in four words.

I have enjoyed a variety of accomplishments as an ARtist through assorted media, creations, ideas, projects and ventures, but through everything it is that one tiny piece of my Life that Fills me with the deepest contentment.

I am an artist.

I say this and smile, and in those First Few seconds when the words are still lingering in the air, my heart Glows a Little Bit Brighter and joy radiates From every cell in my body.

I am an artist.

This is the Greatest treasure; this is the most precious Gift.

This is my Success.

LOVELIEST OF TREES

A. E. Housman

Loveliest of trees, the cherry now
Is hung with bloom along the bough,
And stands about the woodland ride
Wearing white for Eastertide.

Now, of my threescore years and ten,
Twenty will not come again,
And take from seventy springs a score,
It only leaves me fifty more.

And since to look at things in bloom
Fifty springs are little room,
About the woodlands I will go
To see the cherry hung...

In my experiences as a woman who follows her dreams as much as possible, I have been blessed with many dreams come true. I have also had my share of flops and a few dreams made real that reminded me to

be careful about what I wish for.

Through all of this, I have come to believe that there is one element above all others that will have the greatest impact on my ability to not only make a dream real, but to also enjoy it every step of the way:

CERTIFIED MAIL™

expectations.

2434

It is fascinating to explore my past and see all the threads of experience that led me to right now, to see how much it all makes sense... that the foundation of my personality was formed at an incredibly young age and hasn't changed much since then. I have traveled, learned and experienced much, but the essence of who I am and how I live my life is inextricably linked to who I was when I was still running around my house in a costume pretending to be Wonder Woman.

The labels I consisently attach
to myself - Artist
             Wanderer
                Philosopher -

all have their origins in the journey
I started years ago when I would
chase fireflies on warm summer
nights and quench my thirst with a
garden hose, when I needed nothing
more than an empty refrigerator
box and a few crayons to create
my own Magic castle.

I'm still that girl.

And she's just fine, exactly
   the way she is.

STITCH GAUGE: A knitting
to a specified stitch
size, needles with wh
tain the stitch gauge specifi
However, if you do not get
the suggested needle
will give you the spe
at the stitch gauge gi
work to be the size gi

BREVIATIONS

s) . . . .
. . . . stitch (es)
. . . . knit
. . . . purl
this symbol indicates tha
diately following are to be re
of times.

he direction followed

MATERIALS REQUIRE

1 BERNAT Cuddle M
1 pair plastic knitting
or women's sizes
1 pair plastic knittin

GAUGE 7 sts — 2 inches
. . . . 1
3 sts — 1 inch o
. . . . — 1 inch

花京香 はなきょうか

一ヶ月 即日揃え

heate, though you

TO BE LOVED... to travel
through the World and create
a life Beneath a Halo
of Beloved—ness, Beneath the
light created by the act
of Someone maKing a choice
to love you... this is our
Greatest journey.

we have to be willing to let
others into our peculiar little
Worlds to bask under this
exquisite, penetrating light.

It is the day to day that I cherish the most, For it is in those quiet spaces where wisdom is developed and our very selves are created. I have accomplished Great Goals and made Life-Long Dreams come true, but it is not just these experiences that have shaped who I am.

Who I am has also been shaped and sculpted on evenings like tonight, when I had dinner with a girlfriend, gossiped, drank martinis and now sit awake on my own, unable to sleep, with the crickets chirping outside. Grand moments are divine in their own way,

But it is the tiny morsels that make up most of our days that will ultimately define who we are...

The way we interact with a stranger, the tears we cry because someone we love is in pain, the laughter that fills a room, the songs we sing and the smiles we give freely... all the ways we make a positive impact on someone else's life that we are utterly, completely unaware of...

these precious gifts

we give to the world

simply by being

ourselves.

and still still ALive
and can be drawn
options & overwhelmed
fire at our fingertips
from ouizzes
Uncomfortable to
my fears, anxities
comfort zones and fears
a Bomb the world an
Bomb shattered and
Reconfigured Being is
Having is thrilling
unnerving, Shocking
and oh so Beautiful

— Humming Bird

What are your definitions of

SUCCESS?

Are they measured by

* MONEY
* FAME
* CONTROL
* BEING RIGHT
* BEING THE VICTIM

Are your definitions an accurate reflection of your values?

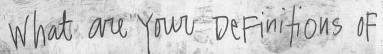

taystitch
ping underlining to top all the way around. At
k edge (A), staystitch ⅝ inch from edge; at coat
n edge (D) and sleeve hem edges (B and C), one

point of gusset.
clip up to corner

If you have pr
will know how

digaban pan y llevaban
A menudo los seguía hasta la puerta del conv
de aquellos monjes era muy viejo; decía que
ordenado San Francisco mismo. Y le

Sometimes we must be willing to Let Go
of that one thing we think Defines us,
that part of ourselves we believe makes us
who we are;
The idea of taking a torch to definitions
we have assigned to ourselves can be
Frightening, but after the destruction,
after the Raging fires that may ensue,
New Growth will always —ALWAYS—
Spring Forth, in places we might
have believed were incapable of
sustaining Life.

when things fall apart, it is time to **rebuild**, and in this moment we have the choice to try to re-create what we had before or start fresh with new materials. In late 2001, when I was in the midst of trying to pick up and re-assemble all the pieces of my life, I was faced with such a choice. After wandering around aimlessly trying to figure out my next steps, I had an epiphany in the oddest of places – in my car on an unremarkable day, at a stop sign in front of the Santa Barbara Mission. For some inexplicable reason – call it a flash of insight or a message from the heavens – a thought came flooding into my brain: it was time to be a GROWN UP. It was time to let go of old ways of being and forge an entirely new path. In that instant, I took my first step.

Until that realization hit me over the head like a coconut, I had been playing the ROLE of a GROWN UP without really embracing it as a key piece of my identity. I had been doing Grown Up things without taking the accompanying responsibilities to heart, trying to be "wise", "sophisticated" and "mature" without understanding that those traits are authentic only when they are embedded in something more fundamental, which is a conscious commitment to being a Grown Up.

Becoming a Grown Up was a decision I made after realizing I had not been doing my best. When so much was lost and I felt unmoored from just about everything I had built my life around, I was compelled to take stock in the choices I had made and the priorities that had been guiding me. This did not mean my heart had to die, that life was no longer fun, or that I couldn't still be wacky and impulsive at times. It meant I took responsibility for my life fully and completely, and made being a Grown Up a grand adventure where anything was possible.

I might have had a laundry list of priorities before this process began, but until I learned how to incorporate them into my day-to-day life, they were nothing more than a collection of balloons tied loosely around my wrist. Like a child at an amusement park, I might have known they were there, but they could be easily ignored as I ran around in a world filled with distractions.

The process of becoming a grown up involved letting go of an old self. As exciting as this was, it also had many sad elements and feelings of profound loss. In the midst of this metamorphosis, I had a vivid dream in which I was attending my own funeral. I sobbed as I saw myself lying in a white casket, and kept reaching in to grab things— a ring, a charm, other small tokens. In the dream I knew I had to say good-bye, but could not control the urge to take the tiny material objects as reminders of who I once was.

When I woke up, I knew immediately this was not a dream about my literal demise, but the death of my former self, a persona that did not fit any more. It was then that I had the bittersweet realization that a part of my life—and perhaps a certain innocence— was gone forever.

NO.1 2 3 45 6 7 8½ 9 10 11

Becoming a Grown Up happened in the midst of tremendous upheaval, but it was during this time of rebirth that I discovered my strongest self and highest priorities. It was a journey of overwhelming responsibility alongside wild freedom, about opening up room in my heart for all the expansiveness and joy I want to create in my life. It was — and continues to be — about HOPE and JOY and Anger and Devastation, and discovering those indestructible parts of myself that have survived it all.

I began this journey by losing my way entirely, and from there, slowly but surely, I made my way back home, back to my most authentic self.

In any endeavor, I say,
"One day at a time,"
and I instantly breathe easier

because this is,
quite simply, the
TRUTH

cheer (chīr) *n.* **1.** Good spirits : gaiety. **2.** Something providing happiness or joy. **3.** A shout of encouragement or applause. —*v.* **1.** To give courage to : hearten. **2.** To fill with happiness. **3.** To encourage or applaud with cheers. **4.** To make or become cheerful <quickly *cheered* up> —**cheer′er** *n.*

Creative community
tribe
soulmates

We all need CHEERLEADERS. We all need supporters who look at us and exclaim, "Yeah YOU!", Going crazy when we score a victory, whatever that victory may be. Supporters who feel deep in their hearts that when you win, THEY WIN. and if you LOSE, they'll keep on cheering, because the most fundamental truth is that you're worth your own CHEERING SQUAD simply by BEING YOURSELF.

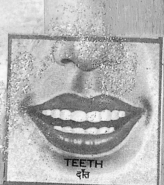

I write, RUN ERRANDS, create and talk on the phone.
I take WALKS, travel, doodle, read and eat takeout Thai Food.
I listen to music, sweep our patio and BUY Flowers
at the Farmer's Market.
        Sometimes I'm totally LaZY.

And it is all part of one Giant CREATIVE STEW,
where the more mixed up I can make things, the
more interesting everything is... where instead of
proclaiming something does not merit the title
"Creative Act", I'll remove the
categories altogether and see
where all those tiny bits of
inspiration and wisdom are
HIDING today, waiting for me to
notice them, usually RIGHT under
MY Nose.

Nothing Fails

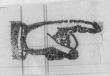

EPILOGUE

I am near the end of this journey, which really isn't an ending, but a doorway to another beginning. As I finish this book, I start to get ready for the release of the book, and that will be an entirely new voyage. This book has been an odyssey made up of many smaller odysseys, and it feels slightly miraculous to have made it this far, with just a few pages left to finish before it is sent off to the printer and returned to me in a more tangible form. Until now, it was just an idea, brought slowly to life as I piled up the finished pages within the walls of my studio over many months. Today marks the day where this vision turns a corner, when I decide with finality the book is complete.

The idea for this book floated in my mind for a long time, and even after I created my first mock-up it sat dormant, stalled by my inability to decide whether or not I should submit it to more publishers after being rejected by an editor that had approached me earlier last year. I was not devastated when this publisher passed on my book; I had accomplished my goal of creating a proposal I was proud of, and once I dropped it in my mailbox I knew its future, at that point, was out of my hands. So it was not disappointment or fear of rejection that caused me to be stuck in indecision for so long, but because I was not sure I had the confidence, strength, energy, ability or resources to pull off self-publishing a full-color 160 page book filled with my own work.

While my ideas and vision sat on a shelf collecting dust, I played a game of tennis in my mind, letting this project volley back and forth between the pros and the cons of self-publishing, submitting to more publishers or just letting it go altogether. Indecision. Doubt. Fear. Wanting to find a way to certainty, to guarantees, to an answer in big bold letters.

This answer came from my past. From taking a Look at what drove me to start SWIRLY in 1995 with a Grand plan and make it a reality over the next decade. In taking a stroll through my own history, my answer became clear — to take on the project myself, to realize my vision on my own terms, to shoulder all the risk, to handle all the details. When I did this for SWIRLY, I soared, and that part of me I thought might have faded away through so many personal and professional changes was right there all along, waiting patiently as I wandered all over the world only to come full circle and make my way back to her.

 *"Hello,"* she said, *"Welcome to your next dream come true."*

And let me tell you — this book is not even finished, has not yet been sent to the printer or seen by another soul in its entirety, but this dream is already real, already bigger than I imagined, already more full of joy and love and beauty than I thought possible. So I am here to say to you that your dreams have power and inspiration far greater than you probably realize, and that the more you are willing to follow them on your own terms, the more the world will be inspired, lifted and enlightened.

In the Final few weeks of finishing this Book, I received an email from an artist I admire whose words Give clarity to this twinkling Light I speak of that shines on the world when we dare to follow our dreams:

Hi Christine...I just had the huge honor of pre-purchasing your hardcover book, and am sitting here in my studio, contemplating a half finished painting, picking up piles of paper, listening to my husband in the other room play his guitar and watch a basketball game on a silent TV, thinking about all the artists out there working, persevering, trying, stretching...and I am smiling. It's not late, maybe 10ish, but it feels like one of those nights at 2am when the world is all at once mysterious and cozy: when ideas and feelings and circumstances all collide and there is that millisecond when it truly feels that anything could happen.

And so here was that millisecond and in a faraway yet real way, you were a part of it, and so as I smiled, listened and felt the moment, I decided to send you a little note, to let you know you were a part of my 2am at 10 in the evening mysterious and lovely millisecond.

Hope your evening is just as lovely....Liz Kalloch

I am inspired everyday By people all over the world, some of whom I talk to every week, many of whom I'll most likely never meet. It is in the stories they tell of realizing a dream, the work they share with the world that is uniquely their own, the passion they cannot help but follow... it is all these things that help me Believe my own dreams are worth tapping into and making a priority.

It is my hope that this Book provides you with the same Kind of Light, a Light that shines Brightly on all the wonder, Beauty and joy you have within you, that will serve the world in so many ways if you dare to expose it BOLDLY, passionately, and confidently.

Blessings...

Christine Mason Miller

Photo of CMM in Boots by Denise Andrade deniseandrade.com
Photos of Blair Beggan & CMM by Gloria Kim
Photo of Four Hands by Susannah Conway unravelling.co.uk
Photo of Melissa Piccola & CMM by Denise Andrade

Photo of CMM by Denise Andrade
Photo of Jen Gray, Denise Andrade, CMM & Andrea Scher
  by Andrea Scher superherodesigns.com
Photo of Kite by Jen Gray jengray.com

Photo Wilited Flowers by Andrea Scher

thank you
MOM

...For Giving me my First sketch Book, For supporting my decision to Be an Art Major, For Following your own dreams and showing me all that's possible...

You are a Light in the World and I am proud to Be your daughter.   I love you... Beanie Blossom

My mom is Suzanne Mason, author of *Be Still My Heart*

bestillmyheart.typepad.com

recognition
APPRECIATION thanks
GRATITUDE
ACKNOWLEDGEMENT PRAISE

Grandma and Grandpa

my family

Mom, who taught me to FLY.

Lawrence, Justin and Taylor
thank you for Giving my Heart a safe Home.

For John Elam... who always sees the TRUTH

MY tribe, MY SOUL SISTERS - MY Creative Community. Without whom I would wither.

Melissa Piccola
Blair Beggan
Andrea Scher, Denise Andrade,
Jen Gray, Marianne
Susannah Conway, Elizabeth
Linda Mechanic, MacCrellish, Marisa Elliott
Haedike, Elyse
Kelly Rae Roberts, Mati McDonough, Frederick,
Heidi Whitney, Helen Webb-Thompson, Kelly Barton,
Sunny Ann Keri Smith, Amy
Schlenger, Howley, Siu.
Penelope Dullaghan,
Christine Castro, Trish Walker,
Mari Robeson, Pixie Campbell
Nicole Fountain

SO MUCH love

Alex & Laurette
Johnston

Johnny & Nancy
Faulkner

Gabe, Tanya,
Katarina, Sofia,
Gaby & Nicolas
Rocha

Carrie, Jim,
Bailey, Ellie, Jack
& Benjamin Garland

For tremendous **support**, ENCOURAGEMENT and JOY
throughout the process of this BOOK and so many other
journeys during my LIFE...

Pilar, Noah, & Paloma Cago
Jon Williams
Mark & Cheri Swank
Dennis & Elizabeth Tito
Brian & Julie Shapiro
Mark DeFilippis
Mary Jo Strack
Pat Piccola
Linda Rosen
Serena Weddle
Mark Hackley
Ginger McCleskey
Dolores Forcino
Cindy Iliff
Katie Camarro
Nina McConigley
Martha Wisbey
Nancy Thompson
Mary Drobny
Lauren Dunn

more Family
Mary Vaughn & Sawyer Matthews

Gus Harper
Joanne Waters
Anne Carmack
Kate Swoboda
Katrina Davenport
Liz Kalloch
Kristen Fischer
M-C Turgeon
Kerstin Martin
Liz Lameroux
Alexandra Saperstein
Joe Cohn
Lisa Laird
Alan Glick & Cathy Lally
Sue Kulesher
Nancy Mills
Icia Farney
Bill Scott
Brendan Searls
Carl Weaver
Trish Huheey
Carol Daly
Alex de Souza

THANK YOU SARK for all the joy you give to the world.

THANK YOU M.A.R.

A very special THANK YOU to DAVID LOEPPKE
For helping to make this Book Perfect.

MAGiSTiR :: www.magistirmusic.com

PUBLISHED IN THE U.S.A.

Miller, christine Mason

Hardcover Edition ISBN 978-0-9818597-0-5
Softcover Edition ISBN 978-0-9818597-1-2

1. inspiration   2. Growth

www.christineMasonMiller.com

FIRST EDITION